BUGS
for
LUNCH

For my adventurous friend Barbara Lucas,
who would not hesitate to eat a well-cooked bug
—M.F.

To my son Matthew, who has always been fascinated by bugs
—S.L.

This edition reprinted by permission of
Charlesbridge Publishing
85 Main Street, Watertown, MA 02472
(617) 926-0329
www.charlesbridge.com

Everyone uses the nickname "bugs" for all kinds of insects, spiders, and other crawly things. There is only one group of insects that scientists consider "true bugs," such as mealy bugs, squash bugs, and others.

Library of Congress Cataloging-in-Publication Data
Facklam, Margery.
Bugs for lunch/Margery Facklam; illustrated by Sylvia Long.
p.   cm.
Summary: Rhyming text introduces bug-eating animals
such as geckos, trout, or even people. Includes additional
facts about each creature.
ISBN 0-88106-271-5 (reinforced for library use)
ISBN 0-88106-272-3 (softcover)
1. Animals—Food—Juvenile literature. 2. Edible insects—
Juvenile literature. [1. Animals—Food habits. 2. Edible
insects.] I. Long, Sylvia, ill. II. Title.
QL756.5.F33   1999
591.5'3—dc21   98-4640

Printed in the United States of America

The illustrations in this book were done in pen and ink and
    Winsor and Newton watercolors on Winsor and Newton
    artist's watercolor paper, 140-pound hot-pressed.
The display type and text type were set in Giovanni.

Designed by Diane M. Earley

With thanks for generous assistance with
illustration references to Peter Menzel and
MAN EATING BUGS: The Art & Science of Eating Insects
by Peter Menzel and Faith D'Aluisio
A Material World Book
Distributed by Ten Speed Press, Berkeley, CA
1998

BUGS
for
LUNCH

Margery Facklam
Illustrated by Sylvia Long

🏛 Charlesbridge

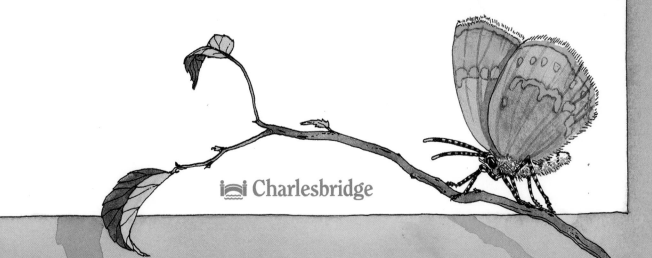

If your lunch was a bug,
Who could you be?
Maybe a nuthatch
At work in a tree,

Or maybe a spider
Trapping a fly,

Or a bat catching bugs
As it cruises the sky.

You might be a gecko

Or maybe a mouse,
Eating the insects
In somebody's house.

You might be a shrew,
Not just eating lunch,
But snacking all day
On bugs by the bunch.

You could be a toad,
Zapping a fly
With a flip of the tongue
In the blink of an eye;

Or maybe a mantis
Ready to prey
On any size insect
That happens its way.

You might be a trout,
At home in a brook,
Looking for insects
That aren't on a hook.

You could be a bear
Searching for honey,
But finding that bees
Taste just as yummy.

Or maybe an aardvark,
Whose tongue, long and sticky,
Slurps termites and ants
That others think icky.

You could be a plant
That can't chase a fly,
But just sits and waits
For its food to drop by.

If your lunch was a bug,
You might be just you,

Munching on insects
As some people do.

More About Bugs for Lunch

There are more insects in the world than any other kind of animal. More than 800,000 insects have been studied and named, but scientists believe that there are probably millions that nobody knows about yet. It's a good thing that insects are food for so many creatures, or the world might be overrun with them.

The *NUTHATCH* is called the upside-down bird because it walks headfirst down tree trunks as it searches for food. With its strong beak, it pries out insects, caterpillars, and insect eggs that are hidden in cracks in the bark.

SPIDERS catch insects in webs and traps made of silk. Each species of spider has a distinctive design for its web or trap. When they catch more than they can eat at one time, most spiders wrap the leftovers in silk to save for a later meal.

BATS fly from their roosts to look for food as the sun goes down. But even in total darkness, they can catch insects. Bats send out a constant stream of sounds that are pitched so high that people cannot hear them. As these sounds hit objects, they echo back to the bat. When an insect flies across this beam of sound, the bat can tell exactly where the bug is and can swoop down to catch it in flight.

A *GECKO* is a small lizard that lives in warm climates. Many people like to have geckos in their gardens and backyards. They know that geckos will come out of hiding at night to eat moths and other insects that people find pesky.

Not everyone likes to have a *MOUSE* in the house because mice nibble on almost anything they can find. Perhaps if more people knew that mice also eat juicy beetle grubs, insect eggs, and moths, they wouldn't mind having a few mice around.

A *SHREW* is one the smallest mammals in the world, and probably one of the busiest. Between short naps, shrews are always on the run, searching for insects. They use so much energy that they cannot go more than a few hours without eating. Every day they eat enough insects to equal two or three times their own weight.

If you find a *TOAD* in your garden, don't chase it away—it's a champion insect eater! A toad's long, sticky tongue is fastened to the front edge of its lower jaw. When a toad sees a bug, it shoots out its tongue, zaps the insect, and has eaten it before you can blink an eye.

A *PRAYING MANTIS* can sit as still as a twig on a tree for hours. When a juicy bug lands nearby, the mantis lashes out and grabs the insect with its spiny front legs. Mantises are welcome in gardens because they eat so many destructive insects. The praying mantis got its name because when it holds its front legs together in front of its face, it looks like it is praying.

When a *TROUT* spots an insect cruising above a brook, it will leap from the cold, clear water and catch the insect in flight. Fishermen often bait their hooks with artificial flies they have made to look like the mayflies and other insects they know trout like to eat.

BEARS aren't fussy eaters. They like all kinds of food—fish, berries, mice, insects, and insect grubs—but they really love honey. When a bear climbs a tree and tears into a beehive with its long claws, bees swarm out. But the bear doesn't seem to mind. Its thick fur protects it from bee stings while it munches juicy bees mixed with the yummy honey.

AARDVARKS, or "earth pigs," live in deep burrows in Africa. They come out of their tunnels at night, when warthogs and their other enemies are sleeping. After an aardvark digs open a huge termite hill or ant nest, it slurps up the swarming insects with its long, sticky tongue.

The *VENUS FLYTRAP* is a carnivorous, or meat-eating, plant. Its hinged leaves are edged with spiny teeth. The slight pressure of an insect landing on a few sensitive hairs on the leaf triggers the leaf to snap shut. In a few days, after the trapped insect has been digested, the leaf opens, ready for another meal to land.

YOU might eat insects, too, especially if you live in a country where meat is scarce. In Cambodia a fat, roasted tarantula is a treat. People who live in central Australia gather moth caterpillars called witchetty grubs to roast in the ashes and hot sand around a campfire. And in Indonesia children use flexible reeds covered with sticky sap to catch dragonflies for a delicious stir-fry served on rice.

around-the-house
HISTORY

WHAT YOU NEVER KNEW ABOUT

TUBS, TOILETS, & SHOWERS

BY **Patricia Lauber**   ILLUSTRATED BY **John Manders**

Simon & Schuster Books for Young Readers

New York   London   Toronto   Sydney   Singapore

You've played hard. Now you're hot, sticky, and dirty.

What could feel better than getting clean all over?

Nearly everyone enjoys it.

Being clean makes you feel good and smell good. But people haven't always thought that bathing was a fine idea. There have even been times when they thought it was sinful. The history of the bathroom in Europe and North America is a strange story of people who washed themselves often, sometimes, or not at all.

A Stone-Age Splash

No one knows when humans first started to bathe themselves. But everybody needs water, at least for drinking, and people of the Stone Age lived beside rivers and lakes when they could. They probably rinsed their hands from time to time.

Perhaps they discovered the pleasures of bathing.

Why you smell funny? Children frightened.

Oops!

During the Stone Age, people did not settle down in one place. They were hunters and gatherers, who moved with the seasons to find food. When they needed to relieve themselves, they just went wherever they happened to be. It was a natural thing to do, and no one felt shy. It is also what a lot of people in many parts of the world have been doing ever since.

The Ancient World: Clean Is In

People have always been willing to walk to get drinking water. But nobody wants to walk miles for a bath. Before people could even think of bathing often, they needed a supply of water. They discovered how to get this through farming.

Starting about nine thousand years ago, people of the Middle East learned to raise food. Farming made it possible to live year-round in one place. And through farming, people learned to control and use water—to store it, to lead it from rivers to fields of crops, and to build drains. As settlements grew, a great idea was born.

> Farmers very clever to move water into field. We very clever too. Why not move water to village?

Having water close at hand made bathing easy. People also found it a pleasure. Over time, almost everyone in the ancient world came to think it was a good idea to be clean.

settlements grew into towns. In some places great civilizations arose. In cities, freshwater flowed through pipes into homes, palaces, and public buildings. Before long the first bathrooms appeared in homes of the rich. Unlike our bathrooms, these were used only for taking baths or showers.

Clean of body, pure of spirit.

The Indus River Valley held one of the world's earliest cities, Mohenjo-Daro. Here miles of underground pipes carried freshwater, while sewers carried away wastewater. Many houses had bathrooms. Beside the temple was a huge public bath used by those who came to worship.

An early toilet in Mohenjo-Daro was made of bricks. Drains carried waste from houses to street gutters, which were linked to an underground sewer.

How many times do I have to tell you? Don't play in the drain!

In Babylon, the rich not only had bathrooms, they had servants to pour water over them. Bathroom floors sloped toward the center, where a drain carried water away. Other people washed themselves in courtyards or in canals.

The bathtub was probably invented in several regions by people who made pottery. A bathtub was really just a big pottery bowl. The earliest known bathtub is about four thousand years old. It was found on Crete in the ruins of a palace. The tub belonged to the queen.

The palace had running water and drains. The tub did not.

The palace had an indoor toilet with a wooden seat, a pottery bowl, and water. A sewer carried away waste.

In Egypt many people bathed at least once a day in the Nile River. Wealthy people had bathrooms, where servants poured water over them.

Crazy!

Rich Egyptians also had toilets. One kind had a wooden seat and a waste jar. Another had a limestone seat. Beneath it was a container of sand, which servants cleaned and changed.

The ancient Greeks thought staying clean was one way to stay healthy. Sometimes a weary traveler was offered a hot bath, with water warmed by the fire. But mostly the Greeks believed in cold baths.

Be a man, my son.

No, no! I'm only a little child.

Pictures on Greek pottery show other ways of bathing.

The Greeks built public baths where they could wash themselves, meet friends, exercise, and talk. The earliest public baths offered cold showers and baths. Later, about two thousand years ago, Greeks could take a hot bath, if they wished.

The Romans also believed in keeping clean to stay healthy. Some Roman houses had bathtubs. But many Romans liked to go to baths outside the home where they could exercise and meet friends.

Most of these baths were private clubs, but some were public. Late in the Roman Empire, the city had hundreds of private baths and eleven huge public ones—the biggest of all could be used by three thousand people at once. Water reached the city through 264 miles of large pipes called aqueducts.

At the baths, everyone went naked—no one was shy.

Enough! Sponge me, oil me, and dry me. I'm meeting friends at a restaurant.

Wood-fired furnaces heated water and air. After exercising, a bather could visit a steam room or even a room with hot, dry air. A warm bath followed. To remove dirt attendants scraped bathers with a curved metal tool, called a strigil.

Strigil

Both Greek and Roman cities had public toilets that could be used by several people at a time. The toilets had stone benches with holes in them. Drains with running water carried away waste. Some houses even had toilets with water to carry away waste. And some people simply threw their waste (and garbage) into the streets.

There was no toilet paper. A sponge on the end of a stick was used for wiping oneself and rinsed in salty water after use.

Greek child
using pottery potty

Roman armies conquered lands as far north as Britain. Wherever the Romans went, they built public baths. But being clean came to an end with the fall of Rome, around the year 476. Fierce tribes from the north and east seized the lands ruled by Rome—and Rome itself.

Beats me. You could walk down the steps.

What is it?

And get all wet? Let's tear it down.

Nearly 1,400 years would pass before Western Europeans thought being clean all over seemed like a good idea again.

The World Beyond Europe: Clean Means Pure

Elsewhere, people were much cleaner than in Europe after the fall of Rome. Some bathed for pleasure, and some for religious reasons. Still others bathed for both reasons.

Muslims are people who practice the Islamic religion. They built beautiful baths wherever they ruled—in Spain, North Africa, and the Middle East.

Turks of the Ottoman Empire built baths like those of the Romans.

In parts of China, rich people had bathrooms. Other people used public baths. Everyone bathed twice a day in cold water.

The Japanese scrubbed and rinsed themselves, then soaked in hot tubs. Bathing was part of their religion, and also relaxing.

Then, as now, the Ganges River in India was sacred to people of the Hindu faith. Bathing in the river was an important religious practice.

The Aztecs built canals and aqueducts that carried water to homes and palaces in their capital city. People bathed often, sometimes using steam baths to become pure of body and spirit.

In North America many tribes bathed in rivers and lakes. The Navajos used steam baths to drive away evil spirits and sickness.

Europe in the Middle Ages: Clean Is Out

Bathing and keeping clean is easy if you have plenty of running water. Without the Roman engineering works, it was hard to keep clean in much of Europe during the Middle Ages, the thousand-year period that followed the fall of Rome. Whole cities grew—but without clean, piped water, baths, or toilets. Open ditches served as sewers that flowed into rivers.

Frequent bathing was also frowned upon during this time. Leaders of the powerful Christian church believed that pleasures of the flesh were sinful—and bathing was one of these pleasures. It was better, they said, to be pure in spirit than clean of body. Some leaders of the Christian church never bathed. But others thought it was good to take a bath every few months.

Some of the cleanest people were monks, men of the Christian faith who spent their lives in study and prayer. They lived together in buildings called monasteries. Monks took baths three or four times a year.

In a monastery, life followed a strict timetable. There were set times for praying, eating, working, studying, sleeping—and for using toilets. And so a monastery had to have many toilets. They were set in outside walls and made of benches with holes. Drains led down the outside of the walls.

Well-to-do people also took baths from time to time. They had servants to do the hard work.

Usually the whole family got in together, while the water was hot. Guests joined the family.

So glad you could join us for a bath.

Pour it in.
Scoop it out.
At least we'll never
End up stout.

Other people did not have bathtubs. If they washed at all, they did so in rivers and streams—in the same water that was used to carry away waste and garbage.

Like the monasteries, castles and big houses had toilets set in walls. Drains emptied into moats or pits. Country people relieved themselves in ditches or behind hedges. In cities, people used the backyard or a quiet corner. At night they used a chamber pot or a bucket. When the pot was full, they dumped it out the window into the street.

Gardez l'eau!

The Renaissance: Clean Is Still Out

The Middle Ages were followed by a time called the Renaissance, when learning, science, and the arts bloomed. A great age of exploration began. But this great age did not cause people to become any cleaner. Many of the natives discovered in the New World were cleaner than the explorers.

Queen Isabella, who gave money to Columbus, had a proud boast: *I have had only two baths in my life: one when I was born and one before my wedding.*

Later, in England, one of the cleanest people was Elizabeth I, who also had a proud boast: *I take a bath once a month, whether I need it or not.* Elizabeth prided herself on having a keen sense of smell. She carried a container of spices to cover up the bad smells around her. There must have been many. Her court seldom bathed. Neither did her subjects.

Sir John Harrington's flush toilet of 1594

A fancy closestool

Chamber pot of 1500

In castles and palaces, people relieved themselves in corners, stairwells, and fireplaces. In their own homes, the well-to-do often used chamber pots hidden beneath padded seats. These were called closestools. Servants removed and emptied the pots. Other people went on dumping chamber pots out windows. Oddly enough, a flush toilet was invented during the reign of Elizabeth, but it did not catch on.

Closestools were not hidden away. They were kept in many rooms. Louis XIV of France even used his as a throne to receive visitors.

Louis also had a huge bath in a splendid room. But if he took a bath, he preferred a small tub in front of the bedroom fire.

Doctors Have Their Say

During the Renaissance, as well as the Middle Ages, many doctors warned against taking a bath. Getting wet, they said, was dangerous to the health. Even so, some well-to-do people visited spas—resorts built around natural hot springs. Many hoped to cure skin diseases and other ills by bathing in the warm waters. No one visited a spa to get clean.

By the late 1700s, doctors still thought healthy people should not bathe. But some thought sick people could be cured by getting wet.

One doctor had his patients walk barefoot in water, on wet grass, or in fresh snow.

To cure disease, many doctors had a patient wrapped tightly in cold, wet sheets. Patients struggled to escape.

The Rain Bath was a shower of icy water.
Doctors liked it. Patients didn't.

Some doctors believed in steam baths. Many home models were invented. This one was used in the United States.

The patients must have been very hardy. They also must have been cleaner than healthy people. But the purpose of a water cure was to get well, not to get clean. No cure called for soap.

The New World: Not Very Clean Either

When Europeans settled in North America, they brought European customs with them. Most rarely took a bath.

Benjamin Franklin was one early American who did take baths. He used a slipper bath, which he had discovered in France.

Other people bathed to get well. In 1799, a Philadelphia woman had a shower in her backyard as part of a water cure. She wrote about it in her diary, saying the shower was "the first time in twenty-eight years that I have been wet all over."

Of course, without servants or running water, taking a bath was a lot of work. Water had to be pumped or drawn from a well, carried in buckets, and then heated.

In the New World, people relieved themselves outdoors. They emptied chamber pots into the streets. Some built an outhouse, which had a pit or a bucket beneath the seat. Emptying the bucket was a job done by younger members of the family.

City streets were filthy with human waste, horse droppings, and garbage. Pigs rooted in the garbage, looking for food.

Indoor Plumbing Finally Returns

By the middle 1800s, changes were starting to take place. Scientists discovered there were tiny living things called "germs" that caused disease. No one could see germs without a microscope. But they were there, breeding in filth, being passed on from person to person. A big cleanup began.

Cities started to pipe in clean water. They built sewers to carry away waste. People without money often used public baths. People with money bought all kinds of baths and showers. At first bathers had to fill their own tubs and pump or pedal or get help to take a shower. Indoor plumbing made a big difference.

Early shower cap

Once houses had running water and drains, inventors designed many kinds of flush toilets.

Fancy early toilet base

Popular flush model

Men's urinal

Indoor plumbing appeared, with hot and cold running water and good drains. Getting clean became much easier. New houses were often built with a special room for bathing and a built-in tub. In 1851, the wife of President Millard Fillmore had the first bathtub with running water installed in the White House.

The Modern Bathroom Is Born

With indoor plumbing came something new—the bathroom as we know it. It was no longer only a place to take a bath or a shower. It became a room with bath, shower, toilet, and basin. At first only the rich could afford bathrooms. But by the early 1900s more and more people had modern bathrooms.

New houses were built with bathrooms. In older houses, a bathroom was made out of a spare room or part of a hallway. Today, bathrooms can be huge or tiny, simple or fancy.

Today, half the people in the world still lack toilets. Many also lack clean water. Those of us who live in wealthy countries are lucky indeed. Most of us have flush toilets and plenty of clean water. And almost all of us enjoy getting wet all over.

BIBLIOGRAPHY

Braudel, Fernand. *The Structures of Everyday Life: The Limits of the Possible.* New York: Harper & Row, 1981.

Brown, Kathryn. "Not a Pretty Picture," *Discover,* January 1998.

*Colman, Penny. *Toilets, Bathtubs, Sinks, and Sewers: A History of the Bathroom.* New York: Atheneum, 1994.

Deetz, James. *In Small Things Forgotten: The Archeology of Early American Life.* Garden City, New York: Anchor Books, 1977.

Dobell, Steve. *Down the Plughole: An Irreverent History of the Bath.* London: Pavilion Books, 1996.

Garrett, Elisabeth Donaghy. *At Home: The American Family 1750–1870.* New York: Harry N. Abrams, 1989.

*Kerr, Daisy. *Keeping Clean: A Very Peculiar History.* New York: Franklin Watts, 1995.

Stern, Philip van Doren. *Prehistoric Europe: From Stone Age Man to the Early Greeks.* W. W. Norton and Company, Inc., 1969.

Stuller, Jay. "Cleanliness Has Only Recently Become a Virtue." *Smithsonian,* February 1991.

Weaver, Rebecca, and Rodney Dale. *Machines in the Home.* New York: Oxford University Press, 1992.

Wilford, John Noble. "Researchers Paint New Portrait of an Ancient People," *New York Times,* February 10, 1998.

Wright, Lawrence. *Clean and Decent: The Fascinating History of the Bathroom and the Water Closet, and of Sundry Habits, Fashions, and Accessories of the Toilet, Principally in Great Britain, France, and America.* New York: Viking Press, 1960.

* indicates a book written for young readers

Artist's Note

After spending time in the library doing research, I begin an illustration with a sketch on layout bond paper using a 2B pencil. I then trace the sketch onto Arches 300-pound hot-press watercolor paper and paint the shadow and color using a combination of Dr. Martin's dyes and Winsor & Newton watercolors. The highlights are added with Winsor & Newton designer's gouache. Finally, I use a black Prismacolor pencil to redraw the sketch on top of the colors. This way, the fun of the sketch is preserved in the final illustration.

SIMON & SCHUSTER BOOKS FOR YOUNG READERS

An imprint of Simon & Schuster Children's Publishing Division
1230 Avenue of the Americas, New York, New York 10020
Text copyright © 2001 by Patricia Lauber
Illustrations copyright © 2001 by John Manders
All rights reserved including the right of reproduction in whole or in part in any form.
SIMON & SCHUSTER BOOKS FOR YOUNG READERS is a trademark of Simon & Schuster.
Book design by Jennifer Reyes
The text for this book is set in Centaur.
Printed in Hong Kong
10 9 8 7 6 5 4 3 2 1
Library of Congress Cataloging-in-Publication Data
Lauber, Patricia.
What you never knew about tubs, toilets, & showers/
by Patricia Lauber; illustrated by John Manders.
p.   cm.
Summary: Describes people's feelings about bathing and methods of keeping clean throughout history, from the Stone Age to modern times.
ISBN 0-689-82420-3
1. Bathing customs—History Juvenile literature. 2. Baths—History Juvenile literature.
3. Bathrooms—History Juvenile literature. [1. Bathing customs—History.
2. Baths—History.] I. Manders, John, ill. II. Title.
GT2845.L39 2001
391.6'4—dc21
99-14517
CIP

#4/0990075

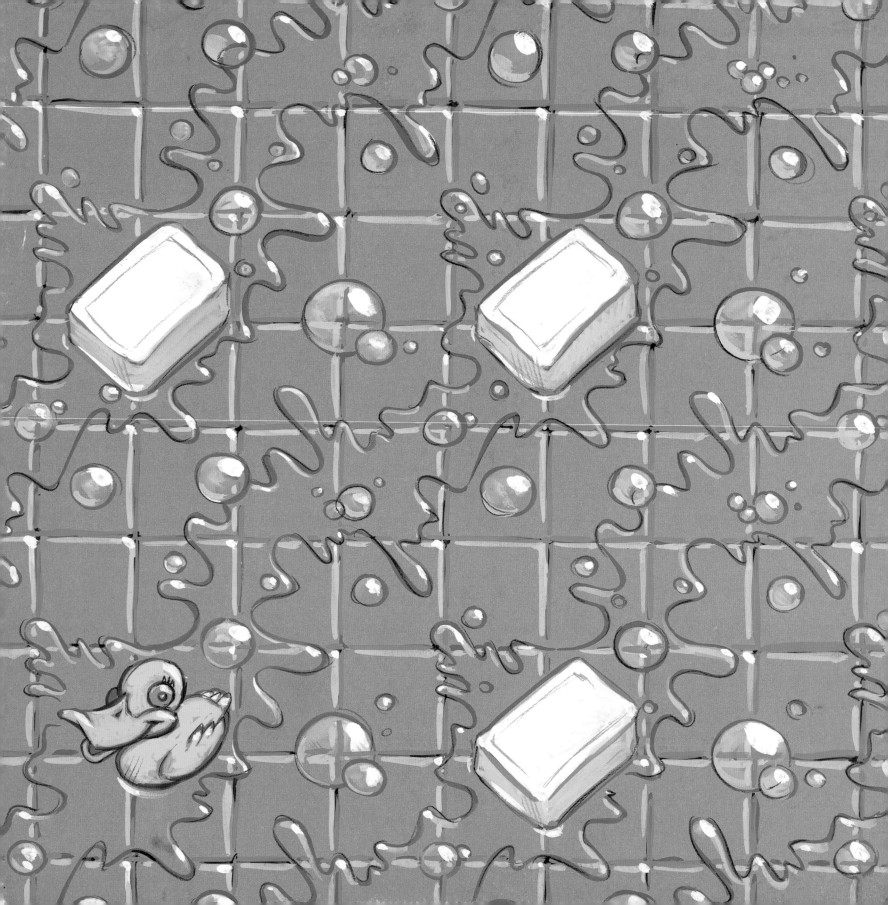